Where Does It Come From?

# From Sand to Glass

by Avery Toolen

Bullfrog Books

# Ideas for Parents and Teachers

Bullfrog Books let children practice reading informational text at the earliest reading levels. Repetition, familiar words, and photo labels support early readers.

## Before Reading

- Discuss the cover photo. What does it tell them?

- Look at the picture glossary together. Read and discuss the words.

## Read the Book

- "Walk" through the book and look at the photos. Let the child ask questions. Point out the photo labels.

- Read the book to the child, or have him or her read independently.

## After Reading

- Prompt the child to think more. Ask: We see and use glass every day. What are some ways you use glass?

Bullfrog Books are published by Jump!
5357 Penn Avenue South
Minneapolis, MN 55419
www.jumplibrary.com

Library of Congress Cataloging-in-Publication Data

Names: Toolen, Avery, author.
Title: From sand to glass / by Avery Toolen.
Description: Minneapolis, MN: Jump!, Inc., [2022]
Series: Where does it come from? | Includes index.
Audience: Ages 5–8 | Audience: Grades K–1
Identifiers: LCCN 2020047892 (print)
LCCN 2020047893 (ebook)
ISBN 9781645279792 (hardcover)
ISBN 9781645279808 (paperback)
ISBN 9781645279815 (ebook)
Subjects: LCSH: Glass manufacture—Juvenile literature. | Sand, Glass—Juvenile literature.
Classification: LCC TP857.3 .T66 2022 (print)
LCC TP857.3 (ebook) | DDC 666/.1—dc23
LC record available at https://lccn.loc.gov/2020047892
LC ebook record available at https://lccn.loc.gov/2020047893

Editor: Eliza Leahy
Designer: Michelle Sonnek

Photo Credits: Shutterstock, cover; Johannes Kornelius/Shutterstock, 1; SchubPhoto/Shutterstock, 3; Pixel-Shot/Shutterstock, 4; BanksPhotos/iStock, 5; nenets/Shutterstock, 6–7, 22tl, 23bl; Morsa Images/Getty, 8–9, 23tl; Svetlana Lazarenka/Shutterstock, 10–11, 22tr, 23tr; DiyanaDimitrova/iStock, 12, 22mr, 23br; donatas1205/Shutterstock, 13; Alba_alioth/Shutterstock, 14–15, 22br; Bloomberg/Getty, 16–17, 22bl; kzww/Shutterstock, 18; Ukrolenochka/Shutterstock, 19; upslim/Shutterstock, 20–21, 22ml; naskami/Shutterstock, 24.

Printed in the United States of America at Corporate Graphics in North Mankato, Minnesota.

# Table of Contents

# Heat and Shape

Sara sips from a glass bottle.

Where does it come from?

# Sand!

sand

Sand goes to a factory.

Materials are added.

factory

furnace

A furnace heats it.

It turns to liquid.

It is cut into globs.

They drop into tubes.

liquid glass

They go in molds.

These shape the glass.

mold

**Glass hardens.**

Flames heat the glass. Why?
If it cools too fast,
it can crack.

Glass is checked for cracks.
It is ready to go!

It is used in many ways.

How?

Bottles hold drinks.

Jars hold food.

Light bulbs and windows are made of it.

Look around!

Where do you see glass?

# From Factory to Home

**How is sand made into glass we can use? Take a look!**

1. Sand goes to factories. Materials are added.

2. It is heated and melts into liquid.

3. Molds shape it. It hardens.

4. The glass goes through flames.

5. It is checked for cracks.

6. We use glass in many ways!

# Picture Glossary

**furnace**
A structure in which heat is produced.

**globs**
Round drops of something soft or wet.

**materials**
Substances from which things are made.

**molds**
Hollow forms in which things are shaped.

# Index

# To Learn More

**Finding more information is as easy as 1, 2, 3.**

❶ Go to www.factsurfer.com

❷ Enter "fromsandtoglass" into the search box.

❸ Choose your book to see a list of websites.